First World War
and Army of Occupation
War Diary
France, Belgium and Germany

52 DIVISION
Headquarters, Branches and Services
Commander Royal Engineers
1 April 1918 - 31 May 1919

WO95/2891/2

The Naval & Military Press Ltd
www.nmarchive.com
Published in association with The National Archives

Published by

The Naval & Military Press Ltd

Unit 10 Ridgewood Industrial Park,

Uckfield, East Sussex,

TN22 5QE England

Tel: +44 (0) 1825 749494

www.naval-military-press.com

www.nmarchive.com

This diary has been reprinted in facsimile from the original. Any imperfections are inevitably reproduced and the quality may fall short of modern type and cartographic standards.

© Crown Copyright
Images reproduced by permission of The National Archives, London, England, 2015.

Contents

Document type	Place/Title	Date From	Date To
Heading	WO95/2891-2 Commander Royal Engineers		
Heading	52nd Division C.R.E Apr 1918-May 1919		
Heading	52nd Divisional Engineers Disembarked Marseilles From Egypt 12.4.18 C.R.E 52nd Division April 1918		
War Diary	Palestine Jaffa	01/04/1918	01/04/1918
War Diary	Ludd	02/04/1918	04/04/1918
War Diary	Ralestine Ludd	04/04/1918	05/04/1918
War Diary	Egypt	06/04/1918	10/04/1918
War Diary	At Sea	11/04/1918	11/04/1918
War Diary	Palestine Ludd	04/04/1918	05/04/1918
War Diary	Egypt	06/04/1918	10/04/1918
War Diary	At Sea	11/04/1918	23/04/1918
War Diary	France	23/04/1918	30/04/1918
Heading	War Diary HQ 52nd (Lowland) Div. RE From 1st May 1918 To 31st May 1918 Vol IV No. 5		
Heading	War Diary HQ 52 Div RE From 1st May 1918 Till 31st May 1918 Vol IV No 5		
War Diary	France	01/05/1918	19/05/1918
Heading	War Diary June 1918 Headquarters 52nd Divisional Engineers Vol 3		
War Diary	France	01/06/1918	28/06/1918
Heading	Headquarters 52nd (Low) Divl. Engineers War Diary July 1918 Volume. IV Part 7		
Heading	Headquarters 52nd. (Low) Divl. Engineers War Diary July 1918 Vol. IV Part 7		
War Diary	France	01/07/1918	31/07/1918
Heading	War Diary Headquarters 52nd. (Low) Divisional Engineers August 1918 Vol. IV No. 8		
Heading	War Diary Headquarters 52nd. (Low) Div. Engrs Vol. IV No. 8 August 1918		
War Diary	France	01/08/1918	31/08/1918
Heading	War Diary Headquarters 52nd (Low) Divl Engineers Vol IV No. 8 August 1918		
Heading	War Diary Headquarters, 52nd (Lowland) Divisional Engineers Volume IV. No.9 September 1918		
War Diary	France	01/09/1918	30/09/1918
Heading	War Diary Headquarters 52nd (Lowland) Divisional Engineers Volume IV No.9 September 1918		
War Diary	France	00/09/1918	00/09/1918
Heading	War Diary H.Q 52nd (Lowland) Div. RE 1st-31st Oct 1918 Vol IV No-10		
War Diary	France	01/10/1918	31/10/1918
Heading	War Diary HQ 52nd (Lowland) Div RE 1st To 31st Oct 1918 Vol No 10		
Heading	War Diary From 1st To 30th Nov 1918 H.Q. 52 Div R.E Vol IV No.11		
War Diary	France	01/11/1918	09/11/1918
War Diary	Belgium	10/11/1918	12/11/1918
War Diary	France	12/11/1918	30/11/1918

Heading	War Diary Headquarters 52nd (Lowland) Divl. Engineers Month Of December 1918 Vol.4 No.12		
War Diary	Belgium	01/12/1918	31/12/1918
Miscellaneous	Report From 52nd Divisional Engineers	07/12/1918	07/12/1918
Heading	War Diary Headquarters 52nd (Lowland) Divl. Engineers December 1918 Vol.4 No.12		
Heading	War Diary Headquarters 52nd (Lowland) Divl. Engineers Month Of January 1919 Vol. 5 No. 1		
War Diary	Belgium	01/01/1919	31/01/1919
Miscellaneous	Casualties For January		
Heading	War Diary Headquarters 52nd Divl Engrs for Month of January Vol V No I		
Heading	War Diary Headquarters 52nd (Lowland) Divisional Engineers For Month Of February 1919 Vol. 5 No.2		
War Diary	Belgium	01/02/1919	28/02/1919
Miscellaneous	Casualties For Month Of February	03/03/1919	03/03/1919
Heading	War Diary Headquarters 52nd. (Lowland) Divl. Engineers For Month Of February 1919 Vol.5 No.2		
Heading	War Diary Headquarters 52nd (Lowland) Divisional Engineers For Month Of March 1919 Vol.5 No.3		
War Diary	Belgium	01/03/1919	31/03/1919
Miscellaneous	Casualties For Month Of March	03/04/1919	03/04/1919
Heading	War Diary Headquarters 52nd (Lowland) Divisional Engineers For Month Of March 1919 Vol.5 No.3		
Heading	War Diary Headquarters 52nd (Lowland) Divisional Engineers For Month Of April 1919 Vol. V No.4		
War Diary	Soignies	01/04/1919	01/04/1919
War Diary	Belgium	01/04/1919	30/04/1919
Miscellaneous	Casualties For Month Of April 1919	30/04/1919	30/04/1919
Heading	War Diary Headquarters 52nd (Low) Divl. Engrs. For Month Of April 1919 Vol. V No. 4		
Heading	War Diary Headquarters 52nd (Lowland) Divisional Engineers Month Of May 1919 Vol. V No.V		
War Diary	Soignies (Belgium)	01/05/1919	31/05/1919
Miscellaneous	Casualties For Month Of May 1919	31/05/1919	31/05/1919
Heading	War Diary Headquarters 52nd (Low) Divl. Engrs. Month Of May 1919 Vol. V No. V		

WO95/2891/2
Commander Royal
Engineer

52ND DIVISION

C. R. E.
APR 1918-MAY 1919

52nd Divisional Engineers

Disembarked MARSEILLES from EGYPT 12.4.18

C. R. E.

52nd DIVISION.

APRIL 1918.

WAR DIARY

INTELLIGENCE SUMMARY

Army Form C. 2118.

HQ 52 Div RE
Vol IV No 4
SHEET 1.

REF MAP PALESTINE
SHEET XIII 1 INCH = 1 MILE

Place	Date	Hour	Summary of Events and Information	Remarks and references to Appendices
PALESTINE JAFFA.	1918 April 1.		Headquarters 52 Div RE at TELAVIV Jewish Colony JAFFA. Hand over all forms and information concerning defences and other works in the JAFFA, SARONA and forward areas to 7th (Indian) Divisional RE. All HQ RE transport equipment complete with weapons, horses and harness were also handed over as above. 410th Field Coy hand over all RE stores in right sector of the line to 7th (Indian) Div. RE. 412 + 413 Field Coys move by march route to Surafend Camp near LUDD and hand over all wagons harness etc to Ordnance – all horses to Remounts and mules driven to Advanced Horse Transport Depot. Lot Coys RE with as much kit and equipment as could be carried in came were not handed in. 412 + 413 Field Coys were reported by their parties to build road being escorted into DIV. RE with tools, being operations on the River JORDAN, and then entrained for KANTARA base to await orders.	
LUDD	2		HQ RE move from JAFFA to Surafend Camp LUDD to await entrainment for the South. 410 Field Coy move from forward area (HADRAH) to SARONA near JAFFA.	
	3		Arrive at ⎯⎯⎯ . KANTARA base and entrain for ALEXANDRIA . 412 and 413 Field Coys arrive at ALEXANDRIA . 413 Field Coy go on board HMT "KINGSTONIAN" but 412 Field Coy go to SIDI BISHR to await embarkation orders. 410 field Coy move to Surafend Camp LUDD to await embarkation for RPN types base.	
	4		413 Field Coy sail from ALEXANDRIA on HMT "KINGSTONIAN" with HMT "MANITO" and an punnia by a convoy of about 20 ships from PORT SAID.	Yes

WAR DIARY / INTELLIGENCE SUMMARY

Army Form C. 2118.

HQ 52nd DIV RE
Vol II No 4
SHEET 2.

Place	Date	Hour	Summary of Events and Information	Remarks and references to Appendices
PALESTINE	1918			
LUDD	April 4.		HQRE and 410 Field Coy Arabs Small Box Respirators. Two Lewis Guns to last Respirators. 410 Field Coy and Lorries to KANTARA and ALEXANDRIA to arms wagons and bivouette pontoon and trestle equipment for the field RE. HQRE Indian Mulla carts horses and 410 Field Coy hand in transport and equipment except Tool Carts toilet equipment proposal as for 412 & 413 Field Coys.	
		5.	412RE and 410 Field Coy leave LUDD for KANTARA.	
EGYPT		6.	HQRE arrive KANTARA also 410 Field Coy who go into camp at General Base depot there	
		7.	HQRE arrive ALEXANDRIA and entrains embark on HMT.	
		8.	HQRE arrive ALEXANDRIA 410 Coy entrain for ALEXANDRIA "INDARRA" 410 Coy entrains for ALEXANDRIA	
		9.	410 Field Co. arrive at ALEXANDRIA and proceed to TRANSIT Camp SIDI BISHR to await embarkation. At this time orders for embarkation of 412 Field Co. had not been given, and special arrangements were instituted for same by C.R.E. as this Coy was expected to proceed oversea with 413 Field Co.	
		10.	412 Field Co. embark on HMT. "OMRAH" and 410 Field Co embark on HMTs "OMRAH" "INDARRA" and "CALEDONIA".	
AT SEA		11.	Convoy of seven Ships including above three sail from ALEXANDRIA. HMT "KINGSTONIAN" with 413 Field Coy aboard was torpedoed in the Mediterranean Sea. No RE casualties but all equipment clothing lost. YOR. left on board as guard on ship now beaching on SARDINIA.	Yes

WAR DIARY
INTELLIGENCE SUMMARY

HQ 52nd DIV RE
Vol II No 4
SHEET 2

Army Form C. 2118.

Place	Date 1918	Hour	Summary of Events and Information	Remarks and references to Appendices
PALESTINE LUDD	April 4.		HQ RE and 410 Field Coy drew Smoke Box Respirators and Tower through Tear Gas to test respirators. 410 Field Coy and Parties to KANTARA and ALEXANDRIA to draw wagons and complete Pontoon Trestle equipment for the Div. RE.	
	6.		HQ RE Pelton mallet cart horse + harness and 410 Field Coy 410 Field Coy entrain and equipment except Tool Carts & train equipment and in transport equipment proprat. as for 412 & 413 Field Coys.	
			HQ RE and 410 Field Coy leave LUDD for KANTARA Base.	
EGYPT	6		HQ RE arrive KANTARA also 410 Field Coy who go into camp at Generalbang Depot there. HQ RE entrain for ALEXANDRIA.	
	7		HQ RE arrive ALEXANDRIA and entrain embark on H.M.T. "INDARRA" 410 Coy entrain for ALEXANDRIA.	
	8		410 Field Co arrive at ALEXANDRIA and proceed to TRANSIT Camp SIDI BISHR to await embarkation.	
	9		At this time orders for embarkation of 412 Field C. had not been given. and Special arrangements were made later for same for CRE. as this coy were expected to proceed overseas with 413 Field Co.	
	10		412 Field Co embark on HMT "OMRAH" and 410 Field Co embark on HMT's "OMRAH" "INDARRA" and "CALEDONIA"	
AT SEA	11		Convoy of seven ships including above three sail from ALEXANDRIA HMT "KINGSTONIAN" with 413 Field Coy aboard was torpedoed in the MEDITERRANEAN SEA the RE personnel but all equipment & clothing lost. TOR. left on board as guard, no ships were treated on SARDINIA	Yes

Army Form C. 2118.

HQ 51st DIV RE
Vol IV No 4
SHEET 3

WAR DIARY
INTELLIGENCE SUMMARY.
(Erase heading not required.)

Place	Date	Hour	Summary of Events and Information	Remarks and references to Appendices
AT SEA	1918 April 12		413 Field Co., which had been taken off H.M.T. "KINGSTONIAN" by the Royal Navy, arrived at MARSEILLES.	
			NOTE: While troops were on sea all ranks stood the standing ships parades and carry out physical exercises and exercises with the Small Box Respirator.	
		14	413 Field Coy entrain at MARSEILLES for ABBEVILLE after partial refit of clothing.	
		17	413 Field Coy arrive at NOYELLES Station and proceed to billets at SAILLY BRAY, where immediate action was taken to refit both with clothing and technical equipment. Others were given further personnel to be trained in route marching, physical training & section drill. This was done pending arrival of arms.	
			HQRE, 410 & 412 Field Coys arrive at MARSEILLES and 410 & 412 Coys proceed to rest camps near the town. HQRE remain on board H.M.T. "INDARRA"	
		18	HQRE entrain & leave MARSEILLES at 0200 for ABBEVILLE. 410 and 412 Field Coys entrain at MARSEILLES and leave for ABBEVILLE.	
		19		
		21	HQRE arrive at NOYELLES and march to RUE. 63rd DIVISION attached to Reserve Army.	
		22	410 Coy arrives at NOYELLES and march to WATHIEHURT. 412 Coy arrives at NOYELLES and march to ARRY.	
		23	All have been in billets and orders for training of Coys especially gas training were issued. This was proceeded with. Pending the arrival of equipment which was received from Field Stores Corps. Those Red been to Field W. Regt. Egyfor by 410 Field Coy.	

Ayoga. Wt. W12839/M1237 750,000. 1/17. D.D & L. Ltd. Forms/C2118/14.

Army Form C. 2118.

HQ 52 Div. RE
Vol IV Nº 4
SHEET 4

WAR DIARY
INTELLIGENCE SUMMARY.
(Erase heading not required.)

Place	Date	Hour	Summary of Events and Information	Remarks and references to Appendices
FRANCE	1918 April 28/29		Companies engaged in drawing and reequipping which were found to be very slow. Equipment on this line drawn from Ordnance MISEVILLE. The delay in drawing transport animals & vehicles or Riding animals, which were drawn from Advanced Horse Transport Depot & Remount MISEVILLE. Animals of reserve rate greatly overworked and attached to 412 Field Coy. Vehicles worn in physique & trained. Staff and Coy had to carry on NCOs and done by this way out efficient instructors.	
	28		HQRE entrained at 7pm for AIRE.	
	29		HQRE arrive at AIRE about 5am and detrain and proceed to BLEWS in the town. 410 Coy entrain at HOTELLES and 412 + 413 Corps entrain at RUE for AIRE.	
	30		All Field Coys arrive at AIRE and 410 + 413 Field Corps proceed to billets in Artillery School, AIRE. Barracks. Work of equipping Field Corps was continued, as at this time animals refused to be about 24/4/18 had not come line and animals detrained to base about 24/4/18 had not come forward. 413 Field Coy had not yet received TOC Carts though these were at ABBEVILLE on 28/4/18. Could could not be drawn owing to move of Coy. Air line arrangements were at once made reference drawing to RE material to RE Division were attached to VI Corps.	Jno

A7092). Wt. w.12839/M1297 750,000. 1/17. D. D & L. Ltd. Forms/C2118/14.

WAR DIARY or INTELLIGENCE SUMMARY

Army Form C. 2118.

HQ 57th/58th RE
Vol IV Sheet No 24
SHEET 5

Place	Date	Hour	Summary of Events and Information	Remarks and references to Appendices
FRANCE	1918			
	April 30		CRE and adjutant at once see Chief Engineer & Staff Officer respectively and all arrangements made for conducts of RE duties. Materials & Stores had work commenced in erection of bayonet fighting gallows, assault courses and repair of shooting ranges & targets at once put in hand. Arrangements made to attach 410 Field Coy and half 412 Field Coy to construct support defences in the Forest of NIEPPE to assist 5th Div. RE. Work carried out under CRE 5th Division. 5th Royal Irish Regiment (Pioneers) to work with Field Corp on above works. This is former battalion which come overseas with 52nd Division from Egypt. GENERAL: Health of troops good, but each weather experienced in France was very trying to all ranks. 2 Units received in France of troops received.	

CASUALTIES FOR APRIL

UNIT	KILLED		WOUNDED		MISSING		SICK TO HOSPITAL		RET'd from HOSP.		REINFORCEMENTS from BASE		HOME LEAVE		RET'd from HOME LEAVE	
	O	OR	O	OR	O	OR	O	OR	O	OR	O	OR	O	OR	O	OR
HQ RE	-	-	-	-	-	-	-	1	-	-	-	-	-	-	-	-
H.D. Field Coy	-	-	-	-	-	-	1	5	-	-	-	11	-	-	-	-
412 Field Coy	-	-	-	-	-	-	1	9	-	-	-	7	-	-	-	-
413 Field Coy	-	-	-	-	-	7*	1	5	-	-	-	4	-	-	-	-
TOTAL	NIL	NIL	NIL	NIL	NIL	7	NIL	19	NIL	NIL	NIL	22	NIL	NIL	NIL	NIL

* Left on board H.M.T. "KINGSTONIAN" see war diary above.

(signed) CRE
adjt 52nd (Lowland) Div RE
57th/58th RE

Vol 2

Confidential.

WAR DIARY

HQ 52nd (Lowland) Div. RE

from 1st May 1918
to 31st May 1918

Vol. IV No 5.

CONFIDENTIAL

WAR DIARY

HQ 52 Bn R.E.

from 1st May 1918
till 31st May 1918

Vol IV No 5.

WAR DIARY
INTELLIGENCE SUMMARY

(Erase heading not required.)

Army Form C. 2118.

H.Q. 52ND Div RE
Vol. IV No 5
SHEET 1.

Place	Date	Hour	Summary of Events and Information	Remarks and references to Appendices
FRANCE	1918 May 1.		HQ. RE in billets in AIRE. H10 and H12 Field Coys moved from billets in Artillery School Barracks AIRE and COHEM respectively to the Forest of NIEPPE about S.F.8.2. and came under orders of GRE 5th Div. H13 Field Coy remain at Artillery School Barracks for month only. Aire and carry on training and recruitment of Company. They are also engaged in maintenance and repair of shooting ranges and around trenches for infantry of the division training in the HAMETZ area.	Ref maps. France Sheet 51a
	2/5		H10 & H12 Field Coys engaged in making MORBECQUE – HAVERSKERQUE defence line for 5th Division.	
	4/5		GRE visited area to initiate Division to enforced to move to for the purpose of reviewing works to be taken over.	
	5		The re-equipment of Field Coys is thought to be unduly delayed and Envoy of mobn lorries is despatched to Ordnance Base CALAIS and considerable consignment Ordnance stores are received. The Canadian RE dumps at ZIVY near NEUVILLE ST VAAST taken over from HQ Canadian Divl Engineers.	
	6		HQRE move by tactical train W 30.6.24. at CHATEAU D'ACQ located W 30.6.24. H10 & H12 Field Coys move from forest of NIEPPE and join Division at Artillery School Barracks AIRE when they go into billets.	Ref maps. 1/20000 MORBECQUE
	7		H13 Field Coy move by tactical train from AIRE to MONT ST ELOY. H10 Field Coy entrain at AIRE for MAROEUIL. H13 Field Coy reliever Canadian Coy R.E. finding 2 sections forward trenches and holding Remainder of Coy at Base Billets.	
	8		H10 Field Coy arrive at MAROEUIL march to MT RIETZ and take over billets from H80 & Z05 FCs JULLECOURT (57th Division) Two sections move forward to take over works north in night sector of Bouvanville line.	Jws

WAR DIARY
INTELLIGENCE SUMMARY.
(Erase heading not required.)

Army Form C. 2118.

HQ 53rd Aus RE
Vol. IV No. 5
SHEET. 3

Place	Date	Hour	Summary of Events and Information	Remarks and references to Appendices
FRANCE	1916 May 15		413 Field Coy. on works in left sector of Honouraine Line, improvements and drainage of trenches, installation of apparatus for dugouts and material to in allow to VIMY village for left sector Battalion's new camp. The forward detachment of the company 413 Field Coy. arrived at Neuville forts and set out and now occupied in these works.	
	16		Brigades in line (right sector) change and 412 Coy. taps over work in this sector from 410 Coy. notice forward detachment move forward to AUX RIETZ and 412 Coy. arms 2 sections forward.	
			RE works now carried out as under:—	
		16/81	410 Field Coy. engaged in sundry small jobs at Corps HQ and making Emergency Officer for Aux Signal Coy. near BtHQ. Maintenance of Aux. Baths at BERTHONVAL and NEUVILLE ST VAAST. Improvement of Reserve Brigade camps in HONT ST ELOY. Improvement repair and camouflage of GREEN LINE trenches & JONATHAN communication trench. Sinking dugouts and making some gun proof & general supervision and checking of materials for Royal Artillery unit's works. Preparation for demolition of various camps and dumps.	
			412 Field Coy. RE work on night section of AUX RIETZ line, drainage camera trap and improvement of trenches, and posts to moving FARBUS and SPUR POSTS with apron fences, inspiration of water storage at FARBUS took 500 gallons at HORDISON dump 500 gallons, at POST LINE near WILLERVAL 600 gallons. These are in tons sought and arrangements	

WAR DIARY
INTELLIGENCE SUMMARY.

HQ. 5TH DIV. R.E. Army Form C. 2118.
Vol. IV N° 5
SHEET. 2.

Place	Date	Hour	Summary of Events and Information	Remarks and references to Appendices
FRANCE	1918 May 8		413 Field Coy entrain at RIKE for ACQ. 417 Field Coy arrive at ACQ and march to billets at A1 Central. Mounted section of all Field Coys H.Q.R.E. transport move by road the following day. Remainder of animals entrained. Tools loaded for night at DIVION where the billeting party and Road reconnaissance were very inferior. Pontoon and trestle equipment of all Field Coys was parked at 1st Army Pontoon Park RANCHICOURT and wagons were converted for use as extra transport for R.E. material. 413 Field Coy Reserve 2 double Tool carts and Reserve G.S. limbers which have been issued in lieu. Field Coys engaged on R.E. works in Divisional area as under:— 416 Infantry on right sector supervising work to 5th Bn Royal Irish Regiment (Pioneers) wiring and fire stepping of THIRD ALLEY. Communication to huts, improvement of GREEN Defence Line near THELUS, improvement and repair of THELUS Road, improvement and drainage of cny communication trenches to sector. The details by the cny billeted at or near THELUS air AUX RIETZ were given training so far as Roadside with side any interference with (proposed) of Sounds. 417 Field Coy: engaged on overhaul of bathing establishments taken over by the Division at BERTHONVAL and NEUVILLE ST VAAST, Sunday improvements at Brit HQ, repair and improvement of Brown Line of Defence.	Refer map MAROEUIL 1/20000 [signature]
	9/II			
	11			
	8/15			

WAR DIARY
INTELLIGENCE SUMMARY

Army Form C. 2118.

HQ. 5th Bn. R.E.
Vol IV No 5
SHEET 4.

Place	Date	Hour	Summary of Events and Information	Remarks and references to Appendices
FRANCE	1918 May 14/31		#13 Field Coy employed R.E. on Eng. works of line; drainage, camouflage and improvement of trenches, repairs and gun emplacements for 155th Infantry Brigade, digging construction of new transport lines, digging new camp for forward detachment of company, erection of bathing ground and await covers for Reserve Infantry Brigade, repair of Lewis shooting ranges, and took forward RE.	
			General works: 1st Canadian Tunnelling Coy RE attached by CE 1st Corps and engaged in making Deep dugouts in Brown defence line and Vimy area.	
		19	The supply of RE material is done by means of our Chief Engineer 1st Corps and thence from 18th Corps RE dumps at MONT ST ELOY (ECOIVRES) or COUPIGNY (CUP). This supply now being maintained with about 2 days supply at RE dumps forward but RE dumps maintained 2 days supply at RIVY near NEUVILLE ST VAAST. From this dump if all material ordered not be used in 2 days were routed to Corps dumps as to and fro none available.	
			Road mines were continuing about 1500 lbs ammonal were taken over from Canadian Engineers Inferior at S.30.c. LES TILLEULS cupboards and Aux RE TR. Special arrangements made for firing these in emergency and for regular weekly inspection by a RE officer.	Ref map 1/2000 photo MAROEUIL
			General: Special attention paid to transport, vehicles all repainted and new unit Div sign pard on vehicles, All lorries three company dumps operated opened of splendid	Jus

Army Form C. 2118.

WAR DIARY
or
INTELLIGENCE SUMMARY.
(Erase heading not required.)

HQ 57 D.M.R.E.
VI Tr A.F.S
SHEET 5

Instructions regarding War Diaries and Intelligence Summaries are contained in F.S. Regs., Part II. and the Staff Manual respectively. Title pages will be prepared in manuscript.

Place	Date	Hour	Summary of Events and Information	Remarks and references to Appendices
FRANCE	1918 May		From forgetting by Trench mortar revetment. Aircraft co-op work carried out at least 2 times in the case of the Lewis guns, but was against limited aircraft ammunition drawn for this and with aircraft mounting's with improvised. Personnel were also trained in the mechanism of the Lewis gun. The Officers and NCO's attended a course on the Lewis gun. Relief during the month: one Officer and two OR being from 410 Siege Bty, all ranks of Green Corp being 2 rounds from Rifle each day for one week as required.

Locations at end of month:
HQ R.E. at CHATEAU D'ACQ — N.30.b.24
410 Siege Bty at AUX RIETZ — A.6.a.3.6
412 " Bosh HQ at — A.1 central
412 " Forward HQ " — S.29.a.95
413 " Back HQ " — F.14.a.34
413 " Forward HQ " — S.29.a.central

CASUALTIES for MAY 1918. | |

	KILLED		WOUNDED		MISSING		SICK TO HOSPITAL		REINFORCEMENTS FROM BASE		HOME ON LEAVE		RETURNED FROM LEAVE		RETURNED FROM LEAVE	
	O	OR	O	OR	O	OR	O	OR	O	OR	O	OR	O	OR	O	OR
HQRE	—	—	—	—	—	—	—	1	—	1	—	1	—	—	—	Justine
410 Coy	—	—	—	—	—	—	—	32	—	8	1	23	1	—	—	3 Capt(rd)
412 Coy	—	—	—	—	—	—	—	13	—	7	1	26	1	1	—	2
413 Coy	—	—	—	—	—	—	1	16	—	12	—	24	1	1	—	3 Capt 62 RS
Total	NIL	NIL	NIL	NIL	NIL	NIL	1	61	—	27	2	74	2	1	—	8 Capt RS

CONFIDENTIAL WAR DIARY. JUNE. 1918.

HEADQUARTERS 52nd. DIVISIONAL ENGINEERS.

WAR DIARY or INTELLIGENCE SUMMARY

Army Form C. 2118.

No. 52nd Div. R.E. Vol IV No. 6. SHEET 1.

Place	Date	Hour	Summary of Events and Information	Remarks and references to Appendices
FRANCE	1917 June 1st to June 5th		**H.Q.R.E.** Located 400 yds West of Bhatow D'acq – W.30.a.3.5. **Hd'qtrs Coy R.E.** employed on the following work:- Labouring Negro area billets, erecting new main Dressing Station, ST. ELOI. (MAROEUIL - 5000 - F.9 & 4H.) marking huts also to proof against bombs at FRASER Camp, FARBUS also to C.O.R.D. erecting huts for D.T.M.O and improving the tram line. Lieut. DEUCHAR R.E. attached to C.E. 2nd Lieut MEDFORTH for work and Lieut GRAHAM BROWN attached to C.E. Company for work. **18th Corps T.M work. 412th Field Coy R.E.** employed on R.E. work in RIGHT Sector of Divisional line, on maintenance of water Dumps at FARBUS, MORRISON and NIKKERVAH. 2 N.C.O's attached to M.G. Battn. for work **43rd Field Coy R.E.** Two sections of the Company at forward position on VIMY RIDGE employed on R.E. work on LEFT sector of Divisional line, erecting ELEPHANT huts at New Brigade Headquarters. Lieut JAS McNAB reported from 552nd A/T. Coy on 5th June and 2nd LIEUT. W.H.T. WANGFORD	

WAR DIARY
or
INTELLIGENCE SUMMARY.
(Erase heading not required.)

Army 1

NR 524 Dn RE
Vol IV N: 6
SHEET 2

Instructions regarding War Diaries and Intelligence Summaries are contained in F. S. Regs., Part II. and the Staff Manual respectively. Title pages will be prepared in manuscript.

Place	Date	Hour	Summary of Events and Information	Remarks and references to Appendices
FRANCE	1918 June 1st to June 8th		WANGFORD left to join 552 A.T. Coy on the 6th June. Work commenced on camouflaged route. From the bottom of HUMBER C.T. to PEGGIE C.T. with a crew to the changing of Brigade by daylight.	
	June 8th to June 15th		410th Field Coy RE At work on repairs to NEUVILLE ST. VAAST Baths. Gas proofing Dugouts in THELUS Rd and R.F.A. Dugouts, also on Camp improvements in Reserve Brigade area. It Hossack and 1 Section detailed for work with R.G. 412th Field Coy RE employed on Drawing and repairing trestles. Repairing and Gas proofing Dugouts. Laying and repairing Duckboards and General R.E work in RIGHT Sector of Divisional line. 413th Field Coy RE Camouflage screen along RED trail completed on the 10th and 156 Bde relieved 155 Bde, a considerable part of the relief being effected by day. C.T. in front of RED and BROWN lines to have blocks - i.e. booths of travers straightened for 40 yards. At work on fixing OLIVER Shrapnel proof	

WAR DIARY
or
INTELLIGENCE SUMMARY.

(Erase heading not required.)

HQ 52nd Div. R.E.
Vol. IV No. 6
SHEET 4.

Army Form

Instructions regarding War Diaries and Intelligence Summaries are contained in F.S. Regs., Part II. and the Staff Manual respectively. Title pages will be prepared in manuscript.

Place	Date 1918	Hour	Summary of Events and Information	Remarks and references to Appendices
FRANCE	June 15th to June 28th		Line/ An ORR's Divisator being erected by this Company, at BERTHONVAL Batts. GENERAL. 1/4 K. NORTHUMBERLAND FUSILIERS (PIONEERS) at work on OTTAWA Trench and improving BROWN line and erecting shelters. 1st CANADIAN TUNNELLING COY employed in making CHAMPAGNE M.G. emplacements and Deep Mined Dugouts in Divisional area – forward of VIMY RIDGE. Two attached Infantry Pioneer Officers and 5 R.E. O.R. attended Gas course at 1st CORPS School, FRESSIN, during month. All O.R. of each Field Coy fired 5 rounds per day for 4 days with S.B.R. on – for practical. Casualties for June 1918	

Casualties for June 1918

	Killed		Wounded		Missing		Sick to Hospital		Reinforcements from Base		Home on leave		Returned from leave		Location of Units during JUNE		
	O.	O.R.	O.	O.R.	O.	O.R.	O.	O.R.	O.	O.R.	O.	O.R.	O.	O.R.	Unit	Locale	
HQ R.E.	-	-	-	-	-	-	-	-	-	4	1	2	-	1	HQ RE	W.30.a.35	Mat.
410 Coy	-	1	-	-	-	-	1	31	1	16	1	16	1	11	410 Coy	A.2.a.56	MARŒUIL
411 Coy	-	3	-	8	-	-	1	9	1	19	1	14	1	30	412 Coy	A.1.central	1/50,000
413 Coy	-	-	-	-	-	-	-	29	-	6	2	15	1	25	de Feria	S.29.a.95	
Total	-	3	-	8	-	-	2	40	2	36	5	47	3	67	413 Coy	F.H.a.34	
															Co Forge	S.29.a.central	

Vol 4

CONFIDENTIAL.

HEADQUARTERS 52nd. (LOW). DIVL. ENGINEERS.

WAR DIARY :- JULY 1918.

Volume.1V. Part. 7.

CONFIDENTIAL.

HEADQUARTERS.

52nd. (Low) Divl. Engineers.

WAR DIARY   JULY 1918.

Vol. IV.   Part. 7.

Army Form C. 2118.

HQ 52nd Div. R.E.
Vol. IV No. Y
SHEET 1

WAR DIARY
or
INTELLIGENCE SUMMARY.
(Erase heading not required.)

Place	Date	Hour	Summary of Events and Information	Remarks and references to Appendices
FRANCE	July 1st 1918		HQRE located 700 yards West of Chateau Dieg. N.30.a.35. HQ 170 Field Coy RE engaged on the following works:- Improving River and field at Mlles HANSON and ST ELOI Camps. Erecting Coy 6 Dumpster North of ELOI. One Section employed on B. Battery work at ATELING. 412 Field Coy RE employed on R.E. work. Right Sector - Dammond line. 413 Field Coy RE Two lectures by a forward section in VOIRT RIDGE - Left Sector - Divisional line. Two sections of VRE work - employed on VRE work - Left Sector - Divisional line. Men of the 1/8th Scott Rifles. 1/5th KOSB. 1/5th A&SH attached to the Catch Improvement Parts at work on Reserve Pilats returned to Reception camp. VINKEAS AU BOIS. to rejoin their Units leaving the Division. One of the shutments at LIM Dump burnt down. One toppedo evacuated to Hospital injured. Two ORRS Disinfectors completed. One at BERTHONVAL and the other at NEUVILLE ST VAAST. The one at NEUVILLE ST VAAST worked very satisfactorily but the other at Berthonval required slight alterations before being put into use.	

WAR DIARY or INTELLIGENCE SUMMARY

Army Form C. 2118.

HQ 52nd Div RE
Vol IV No 7
SHEET 2

Place	Date 1918	Hour	Summary of Events and Information	Remarks and references to Appendices
FRANCE	July 8		First Army Rest Camp opens at AYRESNELLES and 13 OR sent from 52 Div RE to form the nucleus of Junior Officers and Junior NCOs Course an RE border. Two officers and NCOs 8 & 9 Aug. At One at ROUEN. Lieut Bourne and 3 Sergeants.	
	10 to 14		RE's went round left sector (work done on Canadian 3rd Sqn Div) bombing and wiring on Canadian front. Working parties ½ Sqn Div from Canadian bn.	
	15th		RE Canadians & (13 Sqn) took over part of our front sector, the night 13/16 July this included NIKKERWR, TERRUS POST, FARRUS P.S.H. nor SPUR POST	
	20th		R.E. attended conference of CRE's held by D E 8 Corps 413 Field Coy moved into their new billets at BERTHONVAL. Up HANSON camp and built by monos from 156 Brigade, including HQ & field Coy area from Embeaps area to new billets in 14 Corps area.	
			412 Field Coy RE forecast to new at BOIS D'OKHAIN.	
			Q 26 8R F Sheet 44B.	
	23rd		CRE 52 Division takes over works at 12 noon and same Div moves to ENR Reserve	
			HQ R.E. move from CHATEAU D'Ecq to PERNES	
			413 Field Coy RE move from HANSON Camp to LOZINGHEM by train	

WAR DIARY or INTELLIGENCE SUMMARY

Army Form C. 2118.

HQ 5² Can RE
Vol IV No 4
SHEET 3

Place	Date 1918	Hour	Summary of Events and Information	Remarks and references to Appendices
FRANCE	July 23rd		155 Brigade, including H.Q. Field Coy RE. board by march route to new billets in vicinity of Bois D'OHAIN. H.10 Field Coy RE location now P.24.b.4.3. Shot 44b.	
	July 24th		Each Coy has received the additional No of LEWIS Guns, making 5 in all to be carried for Field Coy. Field Coys start intensive training.	
	July 25th		Training — WARE — Musketry	
	July 29			
	July 30th		CRE visits the CRE 4th Canadian Division. H.12 Field Coy move to new billets A.26.d.8.6 MAROEUIL two. H.10 Field Coy move from their billeting area in Bois d'OHAIN including HQ & the 6th Coy RE	
	July 31st		155 Bde Group 1 move from their billeting area in GHQ Reserve by Route march to Canadian O'Able - hence by train to ZINVY dump, and to new billets A.22.d.90 MAROEUIL sheet	
	July 31st		CRE moves to H.Q. 4 Cdn Canadian Engineer Headquarters preparatory to taking over	
	July 31st		H.13 Field Coy RE move from LOZINGHEM to new billets in 4 Canadian Division area preparatory to taking over Centre Sector and are billeted at A.27.c.3.5. MAROEUIL sheet Kovvo.	

WAR DIARY or INTELLIGENCE SUMMARY

Army Form C. 2118.

H.Q. 52nd Div. R.E. Vol SHEET No. 1

Summary of Events and Information

Place: FRANCE
Date: July 1918
Hour: —

Casualties for July 1918.

Unit	Killed O	Killed OR	Wounded O	Wounded OR	Missing O	Missing OR	Sick to Hospital O	Sick to Hospital OR	Reinforcements from Base O	Reinforcements from Base OR	Home on Leave O	Home on Leave OR	Returned from Leave O	Returned from Leave OR
H.Q. 52nd Div RE	—	—	—	—	—	—	—	—	—	—	1	2	—	2
410 (2nd Lo) Field Coy RE	—	—	—	1	—	—	—	12	1	27	1	35	1	33
411 do do	—	—	—	—	—	—	—	11	1	7	1	17	1	21
412 do do	—	—	—	—	—	—	—	8	—	25	1	34	1	34
H.13 do do	—	1	—	—	—	—	—	—	—	—	—	—	—	—
Total	—	1	—	1	—	—	—	31	2	59	4	88	3	90

Location of 52nd Div R.E. at 31/7/18.

H.Q. 52 Div RE. — PERNES — having left F.24.a.9.5. MAP: -
410 (2nd Lo) RE — A.22.d.90 MARŒUIL SHEET 1/20000
411 — do — A.26.d.5.6. — do —
412 — do — — do —
H.13 — do — A.24.c.35. — do —

CONFIDENTIAL.

HEADQUARTERS

52nd. (Low). Divisional Engineers.

AUGUST 1918.

Vol. IV. No. 8.

WAR DIARY.

CONFIDENTIAL.

WAR DIARY.

HEADQUARTERS.

52nd. (Low) Div.Engrs

Vol.IV. No.8.

August. 1918.

Army Form C. 2118.

HQ 52nd Divl RE
Vol IV No 8
Sheet 1.

WAR DIARY
INTELLIGENCE SUMMARY.
(Erase heading not required.)

Place	Date	Hour	Summary of Events and Information	Remarks and references to Appendices
FRANCE	1918 August 1.		Location of 52nd Divl RE. HQ RE at PERNES. 410th Field Co RE " A.22.a.9.0. 412th " " A.26.d.8.6. 413th " " A.27.a.3.5.	Reference maps 1/20000 MARDEUIL
	2.		HQ RE moved from Pernes to MARDEUIL and took over from 4th Brigade Canadian Engineers. All three field Cos went with the line. Dumps at A.13.C. taken over from 4th Bde RE. This sector comprised the front ROCLINCOURT, BAILLEUL and WILLERVAL sectors. Work consisted of drawing and duckboarding and improvement of trenches and communications; repair and gastproofing mined dugouts. Supervision of digging new communication trenches and making new machine gun emplacements for Machine Gun Battalion; construction of new Brigade Head Quarters and alternative alterations to existing HQ. for Infantry Brigades; maintenance of Divisional Rifle Ranges near ROCLINCOURT; construction of small English shelters in trenches; maintenance and extensions to forward water supply system; repair and reconstruction of bathing establishments for the Division in villages of ECURIE and ROCLINCOURT. ROCLINCOURT sector handed over to 51st (Highland) Divl RE and BAILLEUL YWILLERVAL sector handed over to 8th RE. HQ RE moved to MINGOVAL. Dumps at A.13.b. handed over to 8th Divl RE.	

WAR DIARY
INTELLIGENCE SUMMARY

HQ 52nd Div RE
Vol. IV No 8
Sheet 2

Army Form C. 2118.

Place	Date	Hour	Summary of Events and Information	Remarks and references to Appendices
FRANCE	1918 Aug. 16/21		HQ RE at MINGOVAL and Field Corps in surrounding area billeted in Brigade groups engaged in training of personnel and re-equipping.	Ref map LENS 1/100,000
	21		HQ RE moved to HERMAVILLE in preparation for active operations. Field Corps move to LATTRE ST QUENTIN, AGNEZ les DUISANS and HABARCQ.	
	22		HQ RE moved to BRETENCOURT. and Field Corps moved forward into this area in immediate readiness for active operations. Dump of RE materials at R26a taken over from 57 Div RE.	
			HQ RE moved to BLAIREVILLE quarries forward dumps of RE material were formed for operations at M35c25, M35c57, S5a84, S11a39, and N31a16, and at S3c33 as Divisional RE dumps to local reserve of stones to push forward to Field Corps and dumps as required. Ample provision was made in those dumps for wire entanglement material sandbags and all excavation of tools especially digging and mining tools. During active operations Field Corps were engaged in making reconnaissance for water and roads in the battle area and developing water and marking in roads. Road work were engaged in by the 17th Batt. Northumberland Fusiliers (Pioneers) under direction of the CRE. water and road reconnaissance were on the Rivers COJEUR and SENSEE.	

WAR DIARY
INTELLIGENCE SUMMARY.
(Erase heading not required.)

Army Form C. 2118.

H.Q. 52nd Div. R.E.
Vol IV No 8
SHEET 3

Place	Date	Hour	Summary of Events and Information	Remarks and references to Appendices
FRANCE	1918 Aug 26th/30		Parties of R.E. were sent forward with the assault with infantry of the division for the purpose of building blocks in trenches, searching for "booby traps" and mines in the battle area. Road and water development was carried out in the area occupied by GROSVILLE, BOISLEUX and MONT BOISLEUX ST. MARC, BOYELLES, BOIRY BECQUEREL, HENIN, HENIN-Sur-COJEUL, HENINEL, FONTAINES les CROISILLES and CROISILLES X. Communications and water supply were maintained the conclusion of active operations and subsequently, on conclusion of these operations Field Corps and Pioneer Battalion were engaged on road repair work for 17th Army Corps on scheme sent out by the Chief Engineer. The damage to roads was considerable but the Field Corp and Pioneers' work consisted in making the road good for divisional Transport in getting guns, Bridges were repaired to this end. All shell holes were filled in with hard material as surface ceased as far as	

WAR DIARY of INTELLIGENCE SUMMARY.

HQ 52nd Div R.E.
Vol IV N° 8
Sheet 4

Place	Date	Hour	Summary of Events and Information	Remarks and references to Appendices
FRANCE	1918 Aug. 30/30.		Praille. Wells were not usually damaged and not numerous owing to the speed of the operations. Water was found in the Rivers OUSEU and SENSÉE in places on surface and at others by digging to a depth of about 6 to 7 feet. There was no shortage of water or of RE materials for these operations.	Ref 1/20000 map.
	31		H.Q. RE moved from BRAIKEVILLE quarries to T.21.d.8.6 in preparation for active operations towards BULLECOURT. Locations of Field Coys:- 410 Coy at T.5.a.05.05. 412 Coy at T.23.a.8.5. 413 Coy at S.3.c.6.3. General:- The health of the troops was good and the morale excellent. Leave to UK to being granted continuously.	Praille Quarries occpy for RE Stores 3/9/18.

CASUALTIES FOR MONTH OF AUGUST. 1918.

UNIT.	KILLED.		WOUNDED.		MISSING		SICK TO HOSPITAL.		REINFORCEMENTS FROM BASE.		HOME ON LEAVE.		RETURNED FROM LEAVE.	
	O.	O.R.	O.	O.R.	O.	O.R.	O.	O.R.	O.	O.R.	O.	O.R.	O.	O.R.
H.Q. 52nd. Div. R.E.	-	-	-	-	-	-	-	1	-	1	-	2	-	1
410th.(Low). Field Coy. R.E.	-	-	-	4	-	-	-	6	-	16	2	36	1	34
412th.(Low). Field Coy. R.E.	-	-	-	7	-	-	1	17	1	18	-	23	-	37
413th.(Low). Field Coy. R.E.	-	-	-	3	-	1	-	12	-	13	2	34	1	32
TOTAL.	NIL	NIL	NIL	14	NIL	1	NIL	36	1	48	4	95	2	104

Confidential

War Diary
Headquarters
52nd (Lros)
Divl Engineers
Vol IV   N° 8
August 1918

CONFIDENTIAL.

WAR DIARY.

Headquarters, 52nd (Lowland) Divisional Engineers.

VOLUME IV.   No.9.

SEPTEMBER, 1918.

HQ. 52nd Div RE
Vol. IV No 9.
SHEET 1.

WAR DIARY
or
INTELLIGENCE SUMMARY.
(Erase heading not required.)

Army Form C. 2118.

Place	Date	Hour	Summary of Events and Information	Remarks and references to Appendices
FRANCE	1918 Apr 1.		Locations of Div. RE are HQ RE at T21d86 410 Field Coy at T19d88 412 Field Coy at T23a85 (CROISILLES) 413 Field Coy at S3c63	Ref. map. FRANCE SHEET. 1/20000 51B SW.
	17		HQ RE moved to prepared camp in the Hindenburg line D7a.57 near QUÉANT.	
	26		HQ RE moved and answered DHQ in ROBIN SUPPORT line in D28a48 for operations.	
	30		Locations of Div. RE are HQ RE at D28a 48. 410 Field Coy at K6c39 412 Field Coy at D7d87 but move to HOEUVRES same day. 413 Field Coy at E25 b S.H. The work of the Div. RE during this month consisted chiefly in repair and maintenance of roads and the development of water supply. During the active operations at HOEUVRES during the month RE parties carried out the wiring of defences for the infantry and 17th Bn. Northumberland Fusiliers (Pioneers) were used for the	

WAR DIARY
INTELLIGENCE SUMMARY.
(Erase heading not required.)

HQ 52nd Div RE
Vol. IV No 9
SHEET 2.

Army Form C. 2118.

Place	Date	Hour	Summary of Events and Information	Remarks and references to Appendices
FRANCE	1918. Sept.		digging of fire trenches and communication trenches in addition to work on roads.	
			Outline of works.	
			(a) Roads. 410 Field Coy carried out reconnaissance of roads about FONTAINE les CROISILLES, BULLECOURT and towards QUEANT. Repair of road around BULLECOURT. Making broad gauge track from BULLECOURT to QUEANT by HIRONDELLE valley. These roads and tracks are only good for traffic in dry weather. This company was also employed in repair of MOEUVRES – QUEANT Rd. This road is a good metalled and plank road but was considerably cut up before repair. Reconnaissance of 2 aero canals through GRAINCOURT to CANAL D'ESCAUT carried out.	Ref map France
Ref map Sheet 51B S.W. 1/20000
Ref map France Sheet 57cNE 1/20000
			412 Field Coy made a crossing causeway over the CANAL du NORD about E.20.a.8.6 on 27/9/18 and prepared the approaches to same. The infantry did not make this crossing about 10 am and by 1500 this evening cavalry and work of improvements apparatus also being made. This company also	

HQ 52 Div RE
Vol. IV No 9
SHEET 3

Army Form C. 2118.

WAR DIARY
or
INTELLIGENCE SUMMARY.
(Erase heading not required.)

Place	Date	Hour	Summary of Events and Information	Remarks and references to Appendices
FRANCE	1918 Sept.		Carried out considerable improvements in the streets of MOEUVRES and roads leading to this village. 413 Field Coy commenced on 3/9/18 repair of roads in QUEANT, and subsequently were on repair of roads about PRONVILLE and forward. This Coy also prepared tracks for infantry and artillery leading towards the CANAL du NORD. During the operations on this Canal on 27/9/18 the Coy built a trestle bridge over the Canal about E.26.b.7.6. The canal at this point was about 60 feet wide and being unfinished is causing considerable work was entailed in making the approaches to the bridge which was opened for traffic at 6 p.m., work having been commenced on the approaches about 10.30 a.m. On 29/9/18 this trestle bridge was dismantled on the Division moving eastwards. (b) Roads: This was regarded as one of the roots that most importance and considerable effort was made to have abundant development of roads. This was done many horses other than those of the Division being involved at any main points.	Ref map France Sheet 57 NE 1/20000

HQ 5th Div RE
Vol IV No 9.
SHEET 4.

Army Form C. 2118.

WAR DIARY
or
INTELLIGENCE SUMMARY.
(Erase heading not required.)

Place	Date	Hour	Summary of Events and Information	Remarks and references to Appendices
FRANCE	1918 Sept.		410 Field Coy developed water about BULLECOURT, erecting troughs and repairing deep well pump owing to the quick advance wells and lifting gear were found to be very little damaged. This coy made reconnaissance for wells in QUEANT and put down troughs there on 3/9/18 the date on which the Division captured the village Section of the coy were on water development in MOEUVRES and commenced work about 9am on 27/9/18 just after the Divisional infantry had captured the village. 412 Field Coy were in charge of the water development first at CROISILLES and BULLECOURT and later at QUEANT PRONVILLE MOEUVRES. At these places the water was carried on. RE. left Force Pumps were erected at QUEANT where Power Pumps are needed. 412 Coy also reconn- -oitred the water on 3/9/18 at QUEANT and PRONVILLE but development work at the latter place was in hands of 413 Field Coy. Generally it was found that the supply of water was easy in these places which had no difficulty of water supply.	

WAR DIARY
INTELLIGENCE SUMMARY
(Erase heading not required.)

HQ. 52 Div RE
Vol IV No 9.
SHEET. 5.

Place	Date	Hour	Summary of Events and Information	Remarks and references to Appendices
FRANCE	1918 Sept.		**GENERAL:** Works were being carried out near QUEANT, and for 63rd (Royal Naval) Division near ST LEGER. Making Battle H.Q. for 52 Division in ROBIN SUPPORT about D 28 a & 8. Considerable work was done in gasproofing dugouts wherever used by the troops, notably in the PRONVILLE – MOEUVRES area. New H.Q. were made for 17th Corps by enlarging 52nd Div H.Q. at T.01 d (Bullecourt road). When the Division was in support three rifle ranges were made and equipped with targets, making divisional complete. At this time arrangements were made for bathing the Brigades and giving men clean clothing. Training was carried out including range practice as far as work on R.E. services would permit. It is found R.E. are given an inadequate time when the Division is not in the line	By map. France Sheet 57 C N.E. 1/20000

CONFIDENTIAL.

WAR DIARY.

Headquarters, 52nd (Lowland)
Divisional ENGINEERS.

Volume, IV. No. 9.

SEPTEMBER, 1918.

WAR DIARY
or
INTELLIGENCE SUMMARY.
(Erase heading not required.)

Army Form C. 2118.

HQ 52nd Div RE
VOL N° 2
SHEET 6.

Place	Date	Hour	Summary of Events and Information	Remarks and references to Appendices
FRANCE	1918 Sept.		Malcorps: A large German Pioneer dump was found to exist to the north of Malcorps near BULLECOURT. This was taken over by Chief Engineer 17th Corps, and materials supplied from there to the Div. R.E. The Div. R.E. established dumps forward at QUEANT (D7687) and near MOEUVRES (D7612) and from these materials were drawn for active operations. The supply of materials was 9000.	Refmap France Sheet 51B SW 1/20000 Refmap France Sheet 57NE 1/1000

Casualties for September 1918

Unit	KILLED		WOUNDED		MISSING		SICK to HOSPITAL		RET.D FROM HOSPITAL		REINFORCEMENTS		PROCEEDED UK on LEAVE		RET.D FROM UK LEAVE	
	O	OR	O	OR	O	OR	O	OR	O	OR	O	OR	O	OR	O	OR
HQRE	-	-	-	-	-	-	-	-	-	-	-	-	-	-	-	1
W10 Coy	-	1	-	1	-	-	-	16	-	9	-	14	1	37	1	39
H12 "	-	6	-	-	-	-	-	12	-	9	-	11	-	30	-	32
H13 "	-	3	-	-	-	-	-	12	-	5	-	4	-	36	1	30
Total	NIL	NIL	NIL	10	NIL	NIL	NIL	40	NIL	23	NIL	29	2	103	2	108

CONFIDENTIAL

WAR DIARY

H.Q. 52ⁿᵈ (Lowland) DIV RE

1ˢᵗ – 31ˢᵗ Oct 1918

Vol IV No 10

WAR DIARY
INTELLIGENCE SUMMARY.

HQ 52nd Div RE
Vol IV N°10
SHEET 1

Army Form C. 2118.

Place	Date	Hour	Summary of Events and Information	Remarks and references to Appendices
FRANCE	1918 Oct. 1.		HQ RE moved from old British support line at D 28 a 48 to new battle Headquarters near CANTAING Mill. Locations of 52 Div RE. HQ RE at CANTAING Mill. 410th (Lowland) Fd Coy RE at CANTAING. 411th " " " " do. 412th " " " " do. 413th " " " " do. The work in this area was taken over by us from 63rd Divisional RE (Royal Naval) and included the inclined water development in CANTAING, ANNEUX and GRAINCOURT. The supply was from wells and all swirlies were put in order and buckets for raising the water and 600 gallon canvas troughs for water storage were fixed to meet the requirements of the Division. Owing to slowness of raising water by buckets a clutch was installed at GRAINCOURT. This consisted of a large bucket carrying means of 2 mules operating a tackle. This bucket on coming to the well head is tipped and empties the water in trough erected for storage. This solved the difficulty of water supply in large numbers in a short space of time which in large numbers of similar arrangements in FOUR which when the untold supply was taken over	Ref map FRANCE Sheet 1/20000

WAR DIARY
INTELLIGENCE SUMMARY
(Erase heading not required.)

Army Form C. 2118.

HQ SR RE
Oct IV No 10
SHEET 2

Place	Date	Hour	Summary of Events and Information	Remarks and references to Appendices
FRANCE	1918 Oct. 6		HQ RE moved by march route to VAUX-VRAUCOURT. All stores and works in CANTAING area were handed over to 57th Div. RE.	
	7		HQ RE moved by march route to LECAUROY.	
	9		HQ RE moved by march route to BERLENCOURT. CRE to UK on leave and Major B.I. Ridley OC RE @ assumes duty as acting CRE	
	9/19		Period spent as far as possible training Field Coys. This was carried out on programme as far as possible could be adhered to and consisted for dismounted ranks in instruction in infantry drill musketry gas drill &c and for mounted ranks in horsemanship horsemastership stablemanagement "dutie" &c &c. In march discipline great attention was caused to these Considerable interference was caused by the elevenn programme by RE duties called for by the Division such as animeln of rifle ranges targets &c &c and maintenance & better improvements, construction and march route to Chateau d'acq	
	19		HQ RE move by march route to DENIER. Biveronee RE equipment and trades near Arras.	

WAR DIARY
INTELLIGENCE SUMMARY

HQ 52nd Div RE
Vol IV N2 10
SHEET 23

Place	Date	Hour	Summary of Events and Information	Remarks and references to Appendices
FRANCE	1918 Oct 20		HQ RE move by march route to CITÉ ARMAND VOISIN, HÉNIN-LIÉTARD. DCRE podium RE portion RE equipment move from ARRAS to PETIT SAINCY near DOUAI and exchanged over to CE VIII Corps. DOUAI operations and RE are placed at disposal of CE VIII Corps for works. CE 52nd CE 8th Corps and arrange programme of works for the 3 Field Coys. CRE and Adjutant make reconnaissance for Engineers Dumps by Corps about DOUAI, AUBY and COURCELLES and for materials to construct bridges at these places. Tour of captured enemy dumps made. Sufficiency of material was found anywhere found none at CORBEHEM, DOUAI and RAIMBEAUCOURT. Met CE 8th Corps at AUBY. reference site for bridge store. Obtained 3 motor lorries for transport of materials.	Refmap LENS 1/100,000 Refmap VALENCIENNES 1/100,000
	21		HQ RE move by march route from HÉNIN-LIÉTARD to BLANCHE MAISON. CRE & adjutant send recces and arranging further supplies of materials. Made reconnaissance of cross roads for bridges RACHE, ORCHIES, ST AMAND road south of ST AMAND and south towards MARCHIENNES, but	Ref
	22			

WAR DIARY or INTELLIGENCE SUMMARY

Army Form C. 2118.

HOSTROKE
Vol IV No 10
SHEET 4

Place	Date	Hour	Summary of Events and Information	Remarks and references to Appendices
FRANCE	1918 Oct 22		Found these roads impassable owing to demolition by the enemy of all culverts over the numerous feeders in this country. Report on this made to CE 8th Corps	
	23		Railway works Bridge at AUBY completed in 40 hour Roadway. This is triple (timber) bridge to carry 5 Ton axle load (Motor Lorries 6 inch hearts ap). Decking of bridge over railway at DOUAI completed. CRE and adjutant inspected 11th Corps Commander at AUBY Bridge. Instructions to approaches of this bridge removed. CRE to MARCHIENNES to meet O/C 8th Corps reference construction of a bridge over Canal there. This work was not proceeded with as Army Boulogne Officers was commencing work on a Permanent Bridge. CRE Contingent conferred at 156 Inf Bde HQ in AUBY. This was to enquire into circumstances of loss of relins in the Division not connected with R.E. Took commenced on erection of 120 feet Spann HOPKINS girder bridge. HQ R.E. move by march route to FLINES. Took on reconstruction of bridge over Drain on MARCHIENNES-CATELET Road and work on road craters commenced near ORCHIES	VALENCIENNES 1/100,000

WAR DIARY
INTELLIGENCE SUMMARY

Army Form C. 2118.

HQ 52 Div RE
Vol IV No 10
SHEETS

Place	Date	Hour	Summary of Events and Information	Remarks and references to Appendices
FRANCE	1918 Oct 24		Trestle bridge built at RACHES over canal (R32c6.5) This bridge consists of 3 spans each 12 feet, carries 5 ton axle load and was built complete in 11 hours.	Ref map France Sheet 44 1/40,000
	25		CRE inspected to COURCELLES to see erection of HOPKINS bridge in progress and 30 round other works	
	27		Cribpier bridge over stream near ST AMAND station commenced. RE(TF) reconnoitre commenced 412 ft (4 spans) Inglis ORE Crib pier bridge 526 ft erection to span carriageway arranged. Erection of line from JANEON to DROURE CORCELLES bridge launched over canal	
	28			
	29		HOPKINS move by march route to SAMEON (H24) commenced. Reconstruction of culvert at ALLENES under main ORCHIES - ST AMAND road. HOPKINS lattice girder ALEE bridge over canal at PONT á SAULTY near COURCELLES opened for traffic. This bridge is about 100 ft span this carries all (including tanks) way traffic. A tractor and 8 inch howitzer on north carriage at centre open deflected this bridge 1/4 inch. ALLENE culvert referred to above completed	Ref map France Sheet 44 1/40,000
	30			
	31		Cribpier bridge referred to above completed. Work commenced reconstruction of railway raft to ESCAUT (SCHELDT) river and JARD CANAL at K26 and Q5	Ref map Sheet 44 France 1/40,000

WAR DIARY or INTELLIGENCE SUMMARY

Army Form C. 2118.

HQ 52nd Divn RE
vol IV No 10
SHEET 6

Place	Date	Hour	Summary of Events and Information	Remarks and references to Appendices
FRANCE			**GENERAL** In addition to works detailed above the usual domestic works RE have been carried out for the various Inf Bns. Have been employed on road repairs but the service road gradually crept out by the 7th Battalion North Cumberland Fusiliers (Pioneers) and very well carried through under Aux of the OC of this Battalion until the OC of the CRE of the Battn bridging formed an important part of work during the month. The mobile forcing road classes from various Cos by motor lorries and Field Coys hard worked. The design of the structure was made by Bridging Officer and civil engineers and the followed by so 3rd Aux Coys of military conditions allowed after issues of the enemy has rectified several are noted forming to enemy from conversation by opening leaving it at it all remembered the Hospital field remained in any way	

CASUALTIES during Month of OCTOBER, 1918.

Unit.	Killed.		Wounded.		Missing.		Sick to Hospital.		Rejoined from Hospital.		Reinforcements from Base.		Home on Leave.		Rejoined from Leave.	
	O.	O.R.	O.	O.R.	O.	O.R.	O.	O.R.	O.	O.R.	O.	O.R.	O.	O.R.	O.	O.R.
H.Q. R.W.	-	-	-	-	-	-	-	-	-	-	1	-	-	1	-	1
410th Fd. Coy.	-	-	-	1	-	-	-	6	-	2	-	10	-	2	-	38
412th Fd. Coy.	1	-	-	1	-	-	-	11	-	3	2	13	1	1	1	36
413th Fd. Coy.	-	-	-	6*	-	-	-	12	-	5	-	14	-	1	-	36
Total.	1	-	-	7*	-	-	-	29	-	10	2	37	1	5	1	110

* 2 of these Died of Wounds.

3/11/18

J Riolito
Capt RE
adjutant for CRE 52nd (lowland) Division

CONFIDENTIAL

WAR DIARY

(HQ 52nd (Lowland)
A.N RE
1st to 31st Oct 1918

Vol IV No 10

Vol 8

SECRET
WAR DIARY
FROM
1st to 30th Nov 1918

H.Q. 52 Div. R.E
VOL IV no. 11

Army Form C. 2118.

WAR DIARY
INTELLIGENCE SUMMARY.

HQ 52nd Corps R.E.
VOCTV No 11
SHEET 1.

Place	Date	Hour	Summary of Events and Information	Remarks and references to Appendices
FRANCE	1918 Nov 1.		HQ RE at SAMSON (NEUVCONDÉ)	
			110th Field Coy RE at (LOURAINE) I.36.c.6.1 (near LECELLES)	Refugee farmer. Shell nr/near Vicoin
			112th do do at 06.a (LESSAUBOIS)	
			113th do do at F.32.c.35 (VIELLE EGLISE)	
			112th and 113th Field Coys employed in making JERUSALEM-RAFA for crossing of ESCAUT River and JARO canal and in reconnaissance of country for suitable sites.	
			110th Field Coy employed on repair of existing roads in the Divisional Area.	
			412th Field Coy collecting material for heavy (15 ton axle load) timber trestle bridge over ESCAUT and JARO at HERGNIES. This is the existing wheel Gun traffic required in Divisional advance.	
			Carry out in evening JARO and ESCAUT. Enemy retired from JAROG canal front and JERUSALEM Trestle Bridge Thrown across JARO and ESCAUT about R.26.A by 112 Field Coy (Zbridge) and about Q.5.a (4 bridges) by 413th Field Coy. 405 + 413th Field Coys were constructed 2 pontoon Bridges over ESCAUT and JARO at HERGNIES. These were finished and the Rd and Heavy Guns had crossed by midday. Infantry were rested across JARO and ESCAUT by the R.E. immediately the overnight from and construction of bridges went on simultaneously. The operations were successful in face of enormous difficulties occasioned by destruction of the roads by the enemy. On the flooring of fourteen approaches involving 50 to 75 R.E. equipment collision from after afternoon	Nil

WAR DIARY / INTELLIGENCE SUMMARY

Army Form C. 2118.

HQ 5TH DIV R.E.
Vol IV No. 11
SHEET 2

Place	Date	Hour	Summary of Events and Information	Remarks and references to Appendices
FRANCE	1918 Nov 9		HORE road bridge overhead from SAMSON to MONTAU PERUWELZ. 410th Field Coy commences construction of bridge at BLATON. This inclined bridge for firm line transport and motor-transport was designed to carry 6 Ton axle load at 69297, over the canal; construction of bridge to carry 6 Ton of G22550 BRITAINS canal at COOLCHENSLUIS. Already 2 Tons to 2 Tons 6 cwt. axle load. These two were all demolished by 11/11/18.	Reference frame sketch shown
	10		413 RE moved by march route from MONT au PERUWELZ to SIRAULT (I 10).	Reference sketch shown 11/9/1918
	11		413 RE Reccy. commence completion of bridge to carry 6 Ton axle load over BLATON-ATH Canal at STAMBRUGES (H2562) 412 field coy completed bridge (horse timber) at H525M25	
BELGIUM		1100 o'clock	Hostilities ceased	Ref maps Charles 1/40000 1/20000
			Collection of materials in BLATON - STAMBRUGES area carried from enemy dumps where scarcities also Scarcities of materials were found sufficient for the purposes required. Civilian Refugees (by inhabitants 17th North indigenous Industry) (Promos) were employed on repair of roads in this area about HORSIES and forward by PERUWELZ BONSECOURS towards SIRAULT all without hinder a way active in proceeding to employment of officer skilled, opening R.E. Corps B.E.F.	

WAR DIARY or INTELLIGENCE SUMMARY

Army Form C. 2118.

HQ 52 Dn. R.E.
Vol IV no 11
Sheet 3

MAP REF. France and part of Belgium
1/40,000 sheet 45
(except where otherwise stated)

Place	Date	Hour	Summary of Events and Information	Remarks
FRANCE	Nov. 12 1918		Lieut Saroléa 410 Field Coy R.E. became a/adj. in place of Capt. J.L. WHITE proceeding to employment as S.O. to C.E. 8 Corps. B.E.F. **LOCATIONS** H.Q.R.E. SIRAULT I.1.c.3.3. 410 (Lowl.) Field Coy R.E. BLATON 9.9.c. 412 — " — CHAU. DE FORET K 33.d.5.3. (sheet 44 1/40,000). 413 — " — BRUYERE H.7.c. — 410th Fd. Coy. moved to JURBISE p. 22.V.8.8 having completed bridges at G.9.a.9.6, G.15.c.8.9, and G.22.c.8.0 (see Nov. 9th) 412th Fd. Coy. moved to near SIRAULT H.5.c.6.7. 413th Fd. Coy. carried on with construction of heavy trestle bridge over BLATON-ATH Canal in H.2.c. 52nd Div. to be transferred to XXII nd Corps by 15th and then move forward to the RHINE	
	13.		410th Fd. Coy. was engaged in supervising work on the HERCHIES – SIRAULT Road, cleaning hitch, wagons etc and inspecting Rifts. 412th Fd. Coy. overhauled and checked equipment. 413th Fd. Coy. carried on erecting heavy trestle bridge.	

Army Form C. 2118.

WAR DIARY
or
INTELLIGENCE SUMMARY.
(Erase heading not required.)

H.Q. 52. DIV. R.E
Vol. IV no. 11
Sheet 4

Place	Date	Hour	Summary of Events and Information	Remarks and references to Appendices
	1918			REFERENCE MAP. Belgium and part of France 1/40000 sheet 45.
FRANCE	Nov. 14		Traffic passed over bridge in H.2.c. at 1600.	
	15		410 Fd Co. sent 2.O. and 72. O.R. to Mons to take part in formal entry by G.O.C. 1st Army.	
	16		Coys engaged in training and improving roads in the Ouranal area.	
	17		410th Fd. Co. sent 3.O. and 100 O.R. to represent the Divsl. R.E. at a Thanksgiving service held at ERBAUT.	
	18		H.Q. R.E. moved to NIMY. K.32.a.7.6. Coys. engaged in training.	
	19		412th and 413th Fd Coys moved to GHLIN. Training and making Rifle range targets.	
	20		C.R.E. 52 Div. handed over all work west of GRID LINE between I and J. to C.E. 8 Corps except a culvert being repaired on I.14.b. by 17th North'D. FUSRS. Pioneer BN.	
	21		C.R.E. inspected 410 Fd Coy.	
	22		C.R.E. inspected 412 Fd Coy.	
	23		413th Fd. Coy. moved to BRUYERE K.2.c.4.8. Training. 412 Fd Coy. started work on Rifle Range in K.8.a.2.0.	

Army Form C. 2118.

WAR DIARY
or
INTELLIGENCE SUMMARY.
(Erase heading not required.)

H.Q. 52 Div. R.E.
Vol. IV no. 11.
Sheet 5

Place	Date	Hour	Summary of Events and Information	Remarks and references to Appendices
			REFERENCE MAP. Belgium and part of France 1/40.000 sheet 45.	
FRANCE	NOV. 1918			
	24.		Training and work on Rifle Range m.K.8.a.2.0.	
	25.		412 Fd. Co. moved to MASNUY.ST.PIERRE E.14.	
	26.		H.Q. R.E. moved to BRUYERE K.2.C.4.8. 413 Fd. Coy " " MASNUY.ST.PIERRE E.15. held a ceremonial parade C.R.E. inspected 413 Fd. Coy. 410 FD. COY. NERE, DETAILED TO Work proceeded with on Rifle Range B.G.C. 155 INF. BDE. inspected 410 Fd Co. ATTEND	
	27.		52 Div. came under XXII CORPS for administration and is not (at present) going to the RHINE. Training.	
	28.		Training and work on Rifle Range	
	29.		All coys. on route march inspected by C.R.E.	
	30.		17th Bn. NORTH'D FUSRS. (PIONEERS) were employed throughout the month in work on roads and on two further culverts in I.14.6.	

Arthur Sandlea
Lt E2 (T)
a/adj. for CRE 52 Dn.
3/12/18

WAR DIARY or INTELLIGENCE SUMMARY.

(Erase heading not required.)

Army Form C. 2118.

H.Q. 52 DIV. R.E.
VOL. IV no. 11
sheet 6

Summary of Events and Information

Casualties in NOVEMBER 1918

Unit	KILLED		WOUNDED		MISSING		SICK TO HOSPITAL		RETURNED FROM HOSPITAL		REINFORCEMENTS		PROCEEDED U.K. ON LEAVE		RETD. FROM U.K. LEAVE	
	O	OR	O	OR	O	OR	O	OR	O	OR	O	OR	O	OR	O	OR
H.Q.R.E	-	-	-	-	-	-	-	-	-	-	-	-	-	2	-	1
410 COY	-	-	-	-	-	-	1	31	-	7	1	10	-	22	2	29
412 COY	-	-	-	-	-	-	-	7	1	-	1	12	2	17	-	39
413 COY	-	1	-	1	-	-	-	20	-	5	-	6	2	20	1	45
TOTAL	NIL	NIL	NIL	1	NIL	NIL	1	58	NIL	12	2	28	4	61	3	113

John R Baithe
Lt R E
a/adj 52 Div R.E.

3/12/18

CONFIDENTIAL.   WAR DIARY,

　　　　　　　　　HEADQUARTERS.

　　　　　　　　　　　52nd. (LOWLAND) DIVL. ENGINEERS.

Month of DECEMBER 1918.

Vol.4. No. 12.

Army Form C. 2118.

WAR DIARY
or
INTELLIGENCE SUMMARY.
(Erase heading not required.)

Instructions regarding War Diaries and Intelligence Summaries are contained in F. S. Regs. Part II. and the Staff Manual respectively. Title pages will be prepared in manuscript.

Place	Date	Hour	Summary of Events and Information	Remarks and references to Appendices
BELGIUM.	1918. Decr. 1st.		Location of 52nd Divisional R.E.:- H.Q.R.E. BRUYERE, Sheet, 45, K,2,3,5,3. 410th Fd. Coy. R.E. JURBISE, " " " 412th " " " MASNUY St. PIERRE, " " " 413th " " " do do do	
		7th	410th Field Coy., were employed on erecting Water Troughs and Training. 412th " " " " making Rifle Range and in general R.E. work for 156 Bde area. 413th " " " " Company Training, and painted the name of the village, at entrances "MASNUY St. PIERRE".	
			Field Companies employed on Company Training, Cleaning their wagons and equipment, educational training, and on Billet improvement, for their respective Brigades.	
	8th		Major H.T. Davies, M.C. R.E.(T), reported from 6th Division, R.E. and assumed Command of 412th Field Company, R.E. vice Major B.I. Rolling, D.S.O. R.E. (T), promoted C.R.E. 8th Corps Troops.	
	8th/ 12th		Companies employed as on 7th.	
	13th		410th Field Coy. moved by March Route, and are now quartered at LENS, BELGIUM. 413th Field Coy. moved to and take up quarters at LOUVIGNIES.	
	15th		Lieut. J.R. Sartoles, R,E,(T) reported to 410th Field Coy. from H.Q.R.E. where he had been attached as Acting Adjutant.	
	15th		Lieut. G.A. Mitchell, R.E. (T), 413th Field Coy. reported to H.Q.R.E. taking over duties of Acting Adjutant.	
	16th		Lieut. E.B. Dunn, reports from G.H.Q. R.E. Course, at ROUEN, and takes over duties of Adjutant, 52nd (Lowland) Divisional R.E.	
	16th 17th		C.R.E. with A.D.V.S. inspects Horses of Field Companies. G.O.C. inspects Field Companies, with transport, in full marching order.	
	18th to 30th		Field Companies employed on Billet Improvements, Company Training, and Educational Training.	

Vol IV. No 12

Army Form C. 2118.

WAR DIARY
or
INTELLIGENCE SUMMARY.
(Erase heading not required.)

Place	Date	Hour	Summary of Events and Information	Remarks and references to Appendices
BELGIUM.	1918. Dec. 31st		No. 1975, R.S.M. J. Robinson, 52nd Divl. R.E. reports to Divl. Reception Camp, for transfer to England, as a "WATFORD" Detail.	

CASUALTIES FOR DECEMBER.

Unit	Killed		Wounded		Missing		Sick to Hospital		Retd. from Hospital		Reinforce-ments		On Leave to U.K.		Retd. from Leave to U.K.	
	O.	O.R.	O.	O.R.	O.	O.R.	O.	O.R.	O.	O.R.	O.	O.R.	O.	O.R.	O.	O.R.
H.Q. R.E.	-	-	-	-	-	-	-	-	-	-	1	1	-	-	-	2
410th. Fd.	-	-	-	-	-	-	-	21	1	5	-	17	1	12	1	14
412th. Fd.	-	-	-	-	-	-	-	17	-	4	-	6	-	11	-	13
413th. Fd.	-	-	-	-	-	-	1	7	1	7	-	11	1	13	2	12
TOTAL.	-	-	-	-	-	-	1	45	2	16	1	35	2	36	3	41

Lieut. R.E.
Adjut. for C.R.E. 52nd. Division.

7/1/19.

REPORT FROM 52ND DIVISIONAL ENGINEERS.

Chief Engineer,
    XXII Corps.

          Reference E.C. 1074 and S.S. 145.

          It is suggested that the word affiliation in reference to Field Companies should not be used.

          The usual custom and practice by which one Field Company usually works with the same Brigade is excellent and should be followed when convenient. At the same time Field Companies should be independent of Brigades, and the C.R.E. should be able to detail any Field Company to work, with or for any Brigades, as may best suit the circumstances.

          In open warfare great latitude should be left in any Division Orders to the C.R.E. in regard to the movement of Field Companies and Companies of the Pioneer Battalion during operations.

          A considerable degree of freedom must likewise be left to Field Company Commanders to move at their own discretion.

          Field Company Commanders, in mobile warfare, must keep in close touch with Brigade Headquarters when in a Brigade area, or acting with a Brigade.

          During operations, the movement of the Pioneer Battalion should be directed by the C.R.E. direct, except when tactical considerations preclude this.

          The C.R.E. must keep in very close touch with the General Staff.

          The C.R.E. should arrange whenever possible to have some sappers and some pioneers, if only a section and a platoon, up his sleeve to meet rapidly changing contingencies.

          In open warfare except when some definite work, such as the crossings of rivers, are to be dealt with, it is only possible and only desirable to give fairly general orders and directions to Field Company Commanders. The C.R.E. must avoid cramping the style or the initiative of his Company officers. At the same time, the Field Companies must keep in touch with the C.R.E. and must realise the great importance of getting information back to the C.R.E.

          It must be impressed on all Field Company officers that especially in mobile warfare, the R.E. are the servants of other arms, and that in addition to carrying out definite duties or works which have been ordered, the R.E. must be always looking out for opportunities for being useful to the troops, provided Commanding Officers do not attempt to make an improper use of the R.E. or interfere with definite duties which may have been assigned to them by the C.R.E.

          In reference to chapter 4, S.S. 145, the necessary close liaison can be established and maintained by a Field Company with a Brigade, when relations are on a proper footing, without a Field Company Officer being detailed to accompany a Brigadier. Field Companies cannot spare officers in this way.

          It is quite impossible for the C.R.E. to visit Brigade Headquarters daily; neither is it possible or necessary that the C.R.E. should visit daily the Field Company Headquarters.

          When the operations are not too widely extended the C.R.E. and Field Company officers will find means for the necessary interviews without holding conferences.

          In open warfare, one of the principal duties of the R.E. is the development of water. Divisions must rely on their Field Companies for the development of water for troops and animals. Army Troops Coys. and E. & M. Companies are not on the spot in time.

-2-

In the recent advance, the watering arrangements were generally bad because the necessary equipment in the way of light power pumps was not available for immediate installation by Field Companies. There should be available for the C.R.E. at least 2 power driven pumps capable of throwing about 1000 gallons per hour, against a head of 100/120'.

The arrangements, by which, in the recent advance it was the business of the E.& M.Companies to supply and erect engines and pumps, and the business of the Army Troop Companies to provide the distribution by fixing pipes and troughs, were not satisfactory. It was no particular units job to deliver water to the horses in the troughs. Some Divisions appeared to take very little interest in water development, and some appeared to attach more importance to trying to provide baths for men than to provide water for horses.

In dealing with craters it was noted that in many cases where a diversion by timber slabbing was made, this slabbing was laid too much in the form of a semi-circle; the result being that to 6 or 8 horse teams the angle was too sharp and the whole of the teams were not in draft.

Loss of effort occasionally arose after a battle in repairs to roads etc. owing to different people from different units of formations arriving to do the same work. For instance the C.R.E. might have detailed a party of pioneers to fill in certain craters and whilst the work was in progress, parties from Labour Battalions might arrive to do the same work, the result being that far too many men were on the same job and little progress was made.

A box car is absolutely essential for the C.R.E. and without a car it is not to be expected that the R.E. Services of a Division will be really effectively efficiently performed.

(sd) L.FORTESCUE WELLS.
Lieut.Col.R.E.(T)
C.R.E. 52nd (Lowland) Division.

7/12/18

CONFIDENTIAL

WAR DIARY

HEADQUARTERS.
52nd. (LOWLAND)
DIVL. ENGINEERS.

DECEMBER 1918.

Vol. 4.   No. 12.

CONFIDENTIAL.

WAR DIARY.

HEADQUARTERS, 52nd (LOWLAND) DIVL. ENGINEERS.

Month of JANUARY, 1919.

Vol. 5.   No. 1.

Army Form C. 2118.

WAR DIARY
or
INTELLIGENCE SUMMARY.
(Erase heading not required.)

Instructions regarding War Diaries and Intelligence Summaries are contained in F. S. Regs., Part II. and the Staff Manual respectively. Title pages will be prepared in manuscript.

Place	Date	Hour	Summary of Events and Information	Remarks and references to Appendices

BELGIUM.	1919. Janr. 1st.		Location of 52nd Divisional R.E.:-
			     H.Q.R.E. K.2 a.5.3. BRUYERE, Sheet 45.
			     410 Field Co. R.E. LENS.
			     412 " " " " LOUVIGNIES.
			     413 " " " " MASNUY ST. PIERRE.	

	5th.		Companies employed in Company Training, Education, Billet Improvements for Battalions. Men from the Companies being on detachment with various Units.	
	6th.		410 Field Company and 413 Field Company attending practice Ceremonial Drill at JURBISE.	
	7th.		410 Field Company and 413 Field Company attending Ceremonial Drill at JURBISE, presentation of ribbons and inspection by G.O.C.- 2 recipients of M.M. in 410 Field Company.	
	8th.		Companies employed as on 5th.	
	18th. 20th. 23rd. 24th.		Field Companies attend Divisional Inspection by Corps Commander Divisional R.E. Sports. Lieut. Mitchell reported H.Q.R.E. to take over duties of Acting Adjutant. Lieut. Dunn, Adjutant, 52nd (Lowland) Divisional Engineers went on leave to U.K.	
	25th to 31st.		Companies on Training, Education and Billet Improvements. 413 Field Company also on erection of Corps Racecourse.	
			CASUALTIES FOR JANUARY. SEE ATTACHED.	

Army Form C. 2118.

WAR DIARY
or
INTELLIGENCE SUMMARY.
(Erase heading not required.)

Instructions regarding War Diaries and Intelligence Summaries are contained in F. S. Regs., Part II. and the Staff Manual respectively. Title pages will be prepared in manuscript.

Place	Date	Hour	Summary of Events and Information	Remarks and references to Appendices

CASUALTIES FOR JANUARY.

Unit.	Killed		Wounded		Missing		Sick to Hospital		Retd from Hospital.		Reinforcements		On leave to U.K.		Retd. from Leave to U.K.	
	O.	O.R.	O.	O.R.	O.	O.R.	O.	O.R.	O.	O.R.	O.	O.R.	O.	O.R.	O.	O.R.
H.Q.R.E.	-	-	-	-	-	-	-	-	-	-	-	-	1.	-	-	-
410 Fd. Co.	-	-	-	-	-	-	-	8.	-	6.	1.	15.	1.	6.	-	5.
412 Fd. Co.	-	-	-	-	-	-	-	9.	-	11.	-	-	2.	1.	-	-
413 Fd. Co.	-	-	-	-	-	-	1	6	1	8	-	1	1	-	-	1
TOTAL.	-	-	-	-	-	-	1	23	1	25	1	16	5	7	1	6

Tallerhill Lt RE H
a/adj CRE 52 Div

CONFIDENTIAL

WAR DIARY

HEADQUARTERS
52ND DIVL ENGRS

FOR MONTH OF:-
JANUARY

Vol. V
No. I

CONFIDENTIAL

WAR DIARY.

HEADQUARTERS 52nd.)LOWLAND(DIVISIONAL ENGINEERS.

For Month of FEBRUARY. 1919.

VOL. 5. NO. 2.

Army Form C. 2118.

WAR DIARY
or
INTELLIGENCE SUMMARY. Vol. V No 2.
(Erase heading not required.)

Instructions regarding War Diaries and Intelligence Summaries are contained in F. S. Regs., Part II. and the Staff Manual respectively. Title pages will be prepared in manuscript.

Place	Date	Hour	Summary of Events and Information	Remarks and references to Appendices
BELGIUM.	1919 Feb. 1st.		Location of 52nd. Divl. R.E:- H.Q. R.E. K.2 s.5.3. (BRUTIERE, MASNUY St. JEAN) Sheet 45. 410th. Field Coy. R.E. LENS. 412th.Field Coy. R.E. LOUVIGNIES. 413th.Field Coy. R.E. MASNUY St. PIERRE.	
	Feb.1st.		All Coys employed on Education, Billet Improvements etc.	
	Feb. 1st to Feb.24th.		413th. Field Coy. R.E. employed on construction of Race Course for XXII nd. Corps. in addition.	
	Feb. 5th.		Lieut. Colonel L.F. WELLS.R.E. left for DUNKIRK for temporary duty as C.R.E. there, Major STREETEN. 410th.Field Coy. R.E. taking over duties C.R.E. 52nd.Division.	
	Feb. 7th.		Lieut. G.A.MITCHELL R.E.T. A/Adjut. reported to 413th. Field Coy. to proceed to U.K. for Demob. Lieut. J. Mc. Nab 413th.Field Coy. taking over duties as Acting Adjutant.	
	Feb. 10th.		Lieut. RL MASKELL 17th. N. F. (Pioneers) attached to C.R.E. as Education Officer reported to Battalion to proceed to U.K. for Demob. Lieut. T.M. ALLEN 412th Field Coy. reported for duty as Education Officer to C.R.E.	
	Feb. 13th.		A/Capt. DUNN returned from leave from U.K.	
	Feb. 17th.		A/Capt. DUNN Adjutant 52nd. (Low) Divisional Engineers admitted sick to No. 1. C.C.S.	
	Feb. 22nd.		Three Coy. Trestle Equipment supplied to XXIInd Corps Race Meeting as Grand Stand.	
	Feb. 25th. to Feb. 27th. Feb. 28th.		410th and 412th. (Low) Field Coys. as well as 413th. Field Coy. employed in construction of Course for XXIInd Corps Race Meeting. as 1st February to 24th. February.	

28/2/19

James Nunn

Lieut. R.E. T. A/Adjut. for C.R.E. 52nd. Division.

Army Form C. 2118.

WAR DIARY
or
INTELLIGENCE SUMMARY.
(Erase heading not required.)

Vol V No 2

Instructions regarding War Diaries and Intelligence Summaries are contained in F. S. Regs., Part II. and the Staff Manual respectively. Title pages will be prepared in manuscript.

Place	Date	Hour	Summary of Events and Information	Remarks and references to Appendices

CASUALTIES FOR MONTH OF FEBRUARY.

UNIT.	Sick to Hospital.		Reinforcements from Hospital and Base.		On Leave to U.K.		Returned from Leave		To U.K. for Demob.	
	Officers	O.R.	Officers	O.R.	Officers	O.R.	Officers	O.R.	Officers	O.R.
Headquarters. R.E.	1	-	-	-	-	-	1	-	-	2.
410th. Field Coy.	-	4	-	4	-	-	1	2	3	108
412th. Field Coy.	-	2	-	1	-	2	1	2	2	127
413th. Field Coy.	-	-	-	-	1	3	-	-	2	80
TOTAL.	1	6	-	5	1	5	3	2	7	317

3/3/19

James Miller
Lieut. R.E. T.
A/Adjut. for C.R.E. 52nd. (Lowland) Division.

CONFIDENTIAL.

WAR DIARY.

HEADQUARTERS.
52nd. (LOWLAND)
DIVL. ENGINEERS.
for Month of:-
FEBRUARY 1919.

VOL. 5. No. 2.

CONFIDENTIAL.

WAR DIARY.

HEADQUARTERS, 52nd. (LOWLAND) DIVISIONAL ENGINEERS.

For Month of March 1919.

Vol. 5. No. 3.

Army Form C. 2118.

WAR DIARY
or
INTELLIGENCE SUMMARY.
(Erase heading not required.)

Instructions regarding War Diaries and Intelligence Summaries are contained in F. S. Regs., Part II. and the Staff Manual respectively. Title pages will be prepared in manuscript.

Place	Date	Hour	Summary of Events and Information	Remarks and references to Appendices
BELGIUM.	1919 March 1st.		Location of 52nd. Divnl. R.E.:- H.Q.R.E., K.2.a.5.5., Bruyere, Masnuy St. Jean, Sheet. 45, 410th. Field Coy. R.E., Lens, 412th. Field Coy. R.E., Louvignies, 413th. Field Coy. R.E., Masnuy St. Pierre,	1/40,000. do. do. do. do.
	March 1st. to Mar. 13th.		410th. and 412th. Companies employed on Billet improvements in area. 413th. Company employed on further works on Race Course for 2nd. XXII Corps Race Meeting	
	March 13th.		Capt. E.B. Dunn, Adjutant, evacuated from No. 2 Stationery Hospital to U.K. and struck off strength from date.	
	March 14th. to Mar. 21st.		All companies preparing to move to Soignies. Huts at Erbiscoeul and Jurbise being dismantled by 410th. and 413th. Companies respectively, and despatched to Corps R.E. Dump.	
	March 22nd.		H.Q.R.E. and three Field Companies move to Soignies, Location:- Sheet 38, 1/40,000, X.11.a.1.1.	
	March 23rd. to March 31st.		All companies employed on repairs to Billets, erecting Latrines, Spray Baths etc.. Prepared Ramps to entrain wagons and animals. Checking of all equipment and clear A.F.G. 1098 prepared and signed by D.A.D.O.S.	

2/4/19.

[signature]
Lieut. R.E.(T.).
Adjutant for C.R.E. 52nd. Division.

Army Form C. 2.

WAR DIARY
or
INTELLIGENCE SUMMARY.
(Erase heading not required.)

V O L. V. No. 2.

Instructions regarding War Diaries and Intelligence Summaries are contained in F. S. Regs., Part II. and the Staff Manual respectively. Title pages will be prepared in manuscript.

Place	Date	Hour	Summary of Events and Information	Remarks and references to Appendices

C A S U A L T I E S for M O N T H of M A R C H.

UNIT.	Sick to Hospital.		Reinforcements from Hospital, and Base.		On Leave to U.K.		Returned from Leave.		To U.K. for Demobilisation	
	Officers.	O.R.	Officers.	O.R.	Officers.	O.R.	Officers.	O.R.	Officers.	O.R.
Headquarters, R.E.	1*	-	-	-	-	1	-	-	-	-
410th Field Coy. R.E.	-	7	-	7	1	1	1	-	-	14
412th Field Coy. R.E.	-	3	-	1	1	2	-	-	-	10
413th Field Coy. R.E.	-	1	-	1	1	3	-	3	-	12
T O T A L.	1*	11	-	9.	3.	6.	1.	3.	-	36

*This Officer was Evacuated to U.K. on 13/3/19, and struck off Strength.

James Murah

Lieut. R.E.(T).

Adjut. for C.R.E. 52nd (Low) Division.

3/4/19.

CONFIDENTIAL.

WAR DIARY.

HEADQUARTERS.

52nd (Lowland) DIVISIONAL

ENGINEERS.

For

Month of March, 1919.

Vol. 5. No. 3.

CONFIDENTIAL.

WAR DIARY.

HEADQUARTERS &
52nd. (LOWLAND) DIVISIONAL ENGINEERS.

for Month of APRIL 1919.
****

Vol. V.
No. 4.

Army Form C. 2118.

WAR DIARY
or
INTELLIGENCE SUMMARY.

Vol. V.
No. 4.

(*Erase heading not required.*)

Place	Date	Hour	Summary of Events and Information	Remarks and references to Appendices
SOIGNIES. BELGIUM.	1/4/19.		Location, 52nd. (Lowland) Divl. Engineers. Sheet. 58. X. 11. a. SOIGNIES.	
	1/4/19 to 30/4/19.		All Companies engaged on cleaning Wagons, painting and oiling same. Stencilling Coy. Nos etc. on wagons. Making packing cases for Harness and Equipment etc. Stencilling Nos. on same. Inspections of Rifles and Kits. Various minor repairs throughout Divisional Billeting Area.	

Lieutenant R.E. T.
Adjutant 52nd. (Lowland) Divisional Engineers.

30/4/19.

Army Form C. 2118.

WAR DIARY
or
INTELLIGENCE SUMMARY.
(Erase heading not required.)

Instructions regarding War Diaries and Intelligence Summaries are contained in F. S. Regs., Part II. and the Staff Manual respectively. Title pages will be prepared in manuscript.

Place	Date	Hour	Summary of Events and Information	Remarks and references to Appendices
April 1st. 1919.				
			CASUALTIES for Month of APRIL 1919.	

UNIT.	Sick to Hospital.		Reinforcements from Hospital and Base.		On Leave to U.K.		Returned from Leave.		To U.K. for Demobilisation.	
	Officers.	O.R.	Officers	O.R.	Officers	O.R.	Officers	O.R.	Officers.	O.R.
Headquarters. R.E.	-	-	-	-	-	1	-	1	-	-
410th. Field Coy. R.E.	1	-	1	-	2	2	2	3	-	-
412th. Field Coy. R.E.	-	1	-	-	-	2	-	1	-	-
413th. Field Coy. R.E.	-	1	-	1	-	3	1	3	-	1
Total.	1	2	1	1	2	8	1	8	-	1

30/4/19.

Jamenwah

Lieutenant R.E.T.
Adjutant 52nd. (Low) Divl. Engineers.

CONFIDENTIAL.

WAR DIARY.

HEADQUARTERS.

52nd. (Low) Divl. ENGRS.

for Month of APRIL. 1919.
****

Vol. V.
No. 4.

WAR DIARY.

HEADQUARTERS.
52nd. (Lowland) Divisional Engineers.

Month of MAY. 1919.

Vol.V. No.V.

Army Form C. 2118.

WAR DIARY
or
INTELLIGENCE SUMMARY.

VOL. V. No. 5.

(Erase heading not required)

Instructions regarding War Diaries and Intelligence Summaries are contained in F.S. Regs., Part II. and the Staff Manual respectively. Title pages will be prepared in manuscript.

Place	Date	Hour	Summary of Events and Information	Remarks and references to Appendices
SOIGNIES. (BELGIUM).	1/5/19.		Location:- 52nd. (Lowland) Divisional Engineers. Sheet 38 N. X. 11. a. SOIGNIES.	
	1/5/19 to 31/5/19.		Companies engaged on cleaning and Painting wagons etc. Various minor repairs throughout the Divl. Billeting Area. Assisting at Divisional Sports Meeting. Erecting the material required for the Sports Meetings including the launching of the Pontoons and the construction of Rafts for use in the Aquatic Sports Events.	

M. Heatley
Captain R.E.
A/C.R.E. 52nd. (Low) Division.

Army Form C. 2118.

WAR DIARY
or
INTELLIGENCE SUMMARY.
(Erase heading not required.)

Instructions regarding War Diaries and Intelligence Summaries are contained in F. S. Regs., Part II. and the Staff Manual respectively. Title pages will be prepared in manuscript.

Place	Date	Hour	Summary of Events and Information										Remarks and references to Appendices
	May 1st. 1919.		CASUALTIES for Month of MAY 1919.										
				Sick to Hospital.		Reinforcements from Hospital and Base.		On Leave to U.K.		Returned from Leave.		To U.K. for Demobilisation.	
Unit.				Officers	O.R.	Officers	O.R.	Officers	O.R.	Officers	O.R.	Officers	O.R.
Headquarters, R.E.				-	-	-	-	-	2	-	1	-	-
410th Field Coy R.E.				-	2	-	-	1	7	2	2	-	-
412th Field Coy R.E.				-	2	-	1	2	6	-	1	-	-
413th Field Coy R.E.				-	2	-	2	1	7	-	3	-	12
Total.				-	6	-	3	4	22	2	7	-	12
31/5/19.													

M^c^Ath
Captain R.E.,
A/C.R.E. 52nd (Lowland) Divisional Engineers.

WAR DIARY.

Headquarters.

52nd. (Low) Divl. Engrs.

Month of MAY. 1919.

Vol. V. No. V.

www.ingramcontent.com/pod-product-compliance
Lightning Source LLC
Chambersburg PA
CBHW081442160426
43193CB00013B/2361